Flavors of the Beach

TradeWinds Recipes by Chef Jeffrey Fredrickson

TradeWinds
ISLAND RESORTS ON ST. PETE BEACH

Espichel Enterprises, Publishers

TradeWinds Island Resorts on St. Pete Beach, Florida

We are pleased to present our newest book which captures all of our best flavors of the beach.

It features over 100 recipes from our culinary staff, as well a sampling of the flavorful amenities found at our Gulf Coast beach resorts.

Our resorts reflect a variety of tastes, from elegant galas to casual beachfront cookouts...barefoot bistros for tall tropical coolers to sophisticated dining with fresh seafood and aged steaks. Here you may spend days basking in the warmth of the sun...take evening strolls along the seashore...enjoy good times with friends and treasured memories with family.

Discover the classic family-friendly beach resort with a hint of the tropics at TradeWinds Island Grand or experience the tranquility of the more intimate TradeWinds Sandpiper Hotel and Suites. We invite you to enjoy all of our Flavors of the Beach.

Serious meetings are spiced with serious fun, and over 700 guest rooms and suites call you to nights of rest and relaxation. Seven pools and the tranquil Gulf waters refresh your body and velvet white sand beaches restore your soul. Relax in a cabana or a gently swaying hammock, stroll our gardens lush with tropical flowers and palms. At TradeWinds you can... *Just let go*®

Hailing and apprenticing from Massachusetts and a graduate of the Culinary Institute of America, Chef Jeffrey Fredrickson whet his appetite for culinary performance at the Trump Taj Mahal and Castle Casinos in Atlantic City, Grand Bay Hotel in Miami and the Condado Beach Trio in Puerto Rico. Then Chef Jeff found his home in the Tampa Bay area where he became Executive Chef at TradeWinds Island Resorts in 1994.

Overseeing a staff of over 200, Chef Jeff is often found in any one of the resort kitchens making sure that each dish is artfully presented, that each banquet course is a pleasure to the palate and that his busy chefs and cooks are entertained with some very cheerful Boston banter.

First Flavors
Soups, Salads & Appetizers

Crab Bisque en Croute

Red Beard's Seafood Gumbo

Flying Bridge Shrimp & Grouper Chowder

Prickly Pear Duck Breast Salad

Mixed Greens & Goat Cheese Salad

Escargot in Garlic & Pecan Cream Sauce

Crab Croquettes

Pot Stickers

Seared Ahi Tuna

Crab Bisque en Croute

Serves eight

3 shallots, minced

2-1/2 cups clam juice

1-1/2 cups sherry

1 tblsp chopped fresh thyme

pinch of cayenne pepper

1 tblsp paprika

1/2 cup water

3 tblsps cornstarch

2-1/2 cups heavy cream

8 oz picked lump crabmeat

salt & pepper to taste

1 sheet prepared puff pastry

1 egg, beaten

In a heavy bottomed pot, mix shallots, clam juice, sherry, thyme, cayenne pepper, paprika and bring to a boil. Reduce heat and simmer for 3 to 4 minutes. Combine the water and cornstarch until smooth and pour it into the pot, stirring constantly, to thicken. Bring back to a boil. Stir in the heavy cream, bring to a boil again, then add the crab. Season to taste, heat through, remove from heat and let cool. Inverting the soup bowls onto the pastry sheet, cut circles 1/2 inch larger than each bowl. Pour soup into bowls. Brush one side of pastry circles with egg and cover each bowl, pressing the pastry to the sides. Brush tops with egg and bake in a 400° oven for 15 to 20 minutes until well browned. Cook long enough so the tops will not cave in. Serve immediately.

Variations: If you do not wish to serve the bisque en croute, you can simply pour it into soup bowls. Or for a more festive presentation, serve in shot glasses.

Red Beard's Seafood Gumbo

Red Beard's Sharktooth Tavern is our casual beachfront bar and grill serving great seafood gumbo, sandwiches, special pirate rum punches and lots of fun for the entire famly.

Serves six

1-1/2 cups chopped onion
1-1/2 cups chopped celery
2 cups chopped red pepper
1 tblsp minced garlic
3/4 cup margarine
7 cups fish or shrimp stock (page 113)
1/2 tsp each cayenne, black
    & white pepper
1 tsp salt

1/2 tsp dried thyme
1/2 bay leaf
3 tblsps gumbo file
1/3 cup white rice (optional)
1-1/2 cups sliced okra (optional)
1 cup lump crabmeat
12 oz small shrimp, peeled
10 oz scallops
6 bread boules

Saute onion, celery, red pepper and garlic in butter over medium heat for 2 to 3 minutes. Add stock, cayenne, black and white pepper, salt, thyme, bay leaf and gumbo file. If you are including the rice and okra, they should be added at this time. Simmer for 3 to 5 minutes (or 15 to 20 minutes until rice is tender, if added). Meanwhile, gently sift through crabmeat and remove any shells. Add crabmeat, shrimp and scallops to the stock, lower heat and simmer for 6 to 7 minutes until the seafood is poached. Season to taste. Serve in "bowls" created by hollowing out the bread boules.
Note: Steamed rice is generally served on the side, but we add it to our gumbo so that it becomes a one-dish meal served in bread bowls.

Flying Bridge Shrimp & Grouper Chowder

Serves six

1 lb small shrimp, peeled & deveined

1 lb grouper fillets, 1 inch diced

2 cups 1/4 inch diced onion

1 cup 1/4 inch diced celery

1/2 cup salt pork fat (or butter)

1/2 cup flour

6 cups clam juice

1 cup heavy cream

1/4 tsp each white, black
       & cayenne pepper

1-1/2 tsps chopped fresh thyme

1 tsp salt

2 large potatoes

salt to taste

The Flying Bridge at Island Grand is the perfect place for lunch with hearty grilled entrees and tropical drinks at sunset on the beachfront deck.

Saute onions and celery in pork fat over medium heat for 4 to 5 minutes, making sure not to brown. Add flour, stir well and cook for another 3 to 4 minutes. Add clam juice and heavy cream, stirring well, then add white, black and cayenne pepper, thyme and salt. Cook for 10 to 15 minutes over low heat until thickened. If sauce is too thick, add more clam juice. Meanwhile, peel and dice the potatoes into 1/2 inch cubes, then par boil until almost cooked. Add the shrimp, grouper and potatoes to the thickened sauce. Cook for 7 to 10 minutes until the seafood is done. Season with salt to taste.

Serves four

4 duck breasts, 4 to 5 oz each	3/4 cup sugar
vegetable oil	1/4 cup red wine vinegar
salt & pepper to taste	1/2 lb mixed baby greens
4 prickly pears, peeled & cut into chunks	1/2 lb frisee greens
1 tblsp sugar	1 pear, sliced
1 cup water	1/2 pint blackberries

Cook prickly pear chunks in water and 1 tablespoon sugar until soft. In a separate pan cook 3/4 cup sugar until lightly caramelized. Add prickly pear mix and vinegar, then cook until slightly reduced. Strain and set aside. Clean duck breasts and trim off excess fat. Score diamond shapes into the fat sides to help fat rendering. Lightly coat with oil and season to taste. Coat the bottom of a heavy saute pan with oil and heat until very hot. Sear the breasts, fat side down first, for 1 minute on each side. Reduce heat, add prickly pear sauce and cook for 5 to 6 minutes, reducing sauce to a syrup. Remove duck from heat and let rest for at least 5 minutes before slicing. Do not carve hot. Arrange frisee with baby greens and lightly dress with Blackberry Vinaigrette. Drizzle plate with prickly pear sauce and top with duck slices. Garnish with pear slices and berries.

Blackberry Vinaigrette

3 tblsps finely chopped shallots	Puree shallots and oil with one half of the blackberries.
1/3 cup vegetable oil	Dice the remaining berries and stir in with the vinegar.
1 pint blackberries	Mix all ingredients well.
1/4 cup Reisling (or any sweet) vinegar	

Prickly Pear Duck Breast,
Baby Greens & Frisee Salad & Blackberry Vinaigrette

Mixed Greens & Goat Cheese Salad

Serves four

Ginger Tomato Dressing

2 tomatoes
1 tblsp soy sauce
2 tblsps vegetable oil
1 tblsp ground ginger
2 tsps sesame oil
2 scallions, chopped
2 tblsps rice vinegar
2 tsps honey

Blanch the tomatoes in boiling water for 20 seconds or until the skins begin to split, then shock in cold water. Peel, squeeze out seeds, then 1/4 inch dice 1-1/2 tomatoes. Mince the remaining half. Combine with remaining ingredients and mix well.

1 lb mixed spring greens (radicchio, red oak lettuce, baby greens, endive)
5-1/2 oz goat cheese roll (chevre)

5 phyllo sheets
2 tblsps butter, melted
1/3 cup pecans, lightly toasted

Finely chop half the pecans, then rough chop remaining half. Layer phyllo sheets by lightly drizzling two sheets at a time with butter and sprinkling with finely chopped pecans. Top with final phyllo sheet. Top the roll of goat cheese with rough chopped pecans, place next to one edge of phyllo stack, then roll into a 2 inch tube. Crimp ends and bake at 325° for 15 to 20 minutes until browned. While warm, cut into 1/4 inch slices, serve with greens and drizzle with Ginger Tomato Dressing.

Escargot in Garlic & Pecan Cream Sauce

Serves Four

24 Achatin snails	3/4 cup white wine
1 puff pastry sheet	1 cup heavy cream
1 tblsp butter	2 tsps finely chopped fresh parsley
1 tblsp chopped garlic	salt & fresh ground black pepper
1 heaping tsp chopped shallot	petite parisienne (small melon balls)

Puff pastry can be bought in most supermarkets. Cut pastry to desired shape and size, brush tops with eggwash and bake in a 425° oven until puffed and brown. Saute garlic and shallots in butter until they just begin to color. Reduce to medium heat, add wine and reduce to a syrup. Add snails and heavy cream then reduce until slightly thickened. Stir in pecan butter, season to taste and add parsley. Halve pastries, serve escargot over bottom halves and cover with top halves. Garnish with petite parisienne.

Pecan Butter

1-1/2 tblsps butter	Soften butter and mix well
3 tblsps finely chopped pecans	with pecans.

Crab Croquettes   Key Lime Aioli   Sriracha Honey

Serves four

1 lb lump crabmeat	1/4 cup mayonnaise
1/2 red bell pepper, finely diced	2-1/2 tblsps brown mustard
1/4 red onion, finely diced	1 tblsp horseradish
1 tsp chopped garlic	dash of crushed red pepper
1/2 stalk celery, finely diced	dash of dried thyme
2 tblsps canola or olive oil	kosher salt to taste
2 tblsps chopped fresh cilantro	2 tblsps butter
2 tblsps chopped fresh parsley	1 cup panko bread crumbs

Gently sift through crabmeat, removing any shells. Saute pepper, onion, garlic and celery in oil then let cool. Combine with remaining ingredients, except butter and bread crumbs, in a stainless steel bowl. Scoop and shape into 8 balls, lightly press in bread crumbs and saute in butter over medium heat until golden on each side. Serve with Key Lime Aioli and Sriracha Honey.

Sriracha Honey

1/2 tblsp sriracha
2 tblsps honey
1 tsp lemon juice
2 tsps water
pinch of kosher salt & pepper

Stir all ingredients together until well combined. Drizzle over crab cakes.

Key Lime Aioli

1 cup mayonnaise	crushed red pepper to taste
1/4 cup sour cream	kosher salt & pepper to taste
1/2 cup Key lime juice	2-1/2 tblsps extra virgin olive oil
1 tsp chopped garlic	

Whisk all ingredients, except the olive oil, together in a bowl. Whisk in the oil, serve or refrigerate for up to a week.

Pot Stickers

Makes approximately 3 dozen

Filling

3/4 cup ground pork

1/2 cup minced raw shrimp meat

1 cup finely diced cabbage

2 shiitake mushrooms, julienned

1/2 tsp sesame oil

2 tblsps soy sauce

2 tblsps chopped fresh cilantro

1 tsp chopped fresh ginger

1/2 tsp salt & pepper to taste

Combine all ingredients and mix well. Pork and shrimp are the traditional mix, but lobster may also be used. Any of the three can be used in any combination or alone.

1 lb won ton skins or gyoza skins,
   (round) found in Asian markets

1 egg, beaten

vegetable oil

1/2 cup water

If using won ton skins, cut into circles. Brush one side with egg and place 1 heaping teaspoon of filling in center. Fold in half and pinch edges together, making pleats as necessary. In a large non-stick pan lightly coated with oil, saute over medium high heat until the bottoms are browned (shake pan occasionally to avoid sticking). Add water, cover and steam for 1 to 2 minutes until outside edges are transparent. Serve with Dipping Sauce page (112).

Serves Four

4 Ahi tuna fillets, 3 oz each	1 roasted red pepper (page 56)
2 tblsps black & white sesame seeds	1/2 cup Wakame seaweed salad
1/2 tsp kosher salt	1/2 medium onion, shredded
2 tblsps olive oil	seasoned flour
1/2 mango, cut into 1/4" slices	peanut oil for frying

Peel, seed and julienne the red pepper. Grill the mango slices for 2 minutes on each side until caramelized. Coat the shredded onion with flour seasoned with salt, pepper, paprika and chili powder. Deep fry in peanut oil until light brown and crispy.

Coat tuna fillets with sesame seeds and season with kosher salt. Heat olive oil in a cast iron skillet until almost smoking and sear tuna for 1 minute on each side being careful not to overload pan. Remove from heat and let rest.

Wasabi Sauce

6 tsps wasabi powder
7 tsps water
1 tsp soy sauce
1 tblsp sour cream

Mix all ingredients until smooth and lump free.

Drizzle plates with Wasabi Sauce, top with sliced tuna, seaweed salad and red pepper. Garnish with mango slices.

Note: Wakame seaweed salad is available in most supermarkets where fresh sushi is made.

Seared Ahi Tuna

There is an easy, island-like ambiance at the TradeWinds Resorts that almost demands that guests kick back, let go and enjoy a relaxed vacation, from sunning on our Gulf of Mexico beach or cruising along our waterway, to dining in one of our fine restaurants. TradeWinds' unique location provides more than just a wonderful place to vacation. A variety of exciting venues takes advantage of our spectacular tropical climate and beautiful beaches for special events, memorable celebrations, and of course, serious business meetings.

Palm Court Bistro at Island Grand boasts artfully prepared meals by Chef Justin Harry. After discovering the art of cooking in Italy, Chef Justin joined the Trade Winds staff in 1994. While favoring classic European cuisine, he enhances his traditional offerings with eclectic, fusion dishes and inventive nightly specials.

Chef Michael Rabidoux started his career at TradeWinds. Inspired by Chef Jeff, he graduated from the Culinary Institute of America, then returned to the resort to lend his creativity to the Bermudas menu. His Caribe-inspired seafood and exceptional aged Black Angus steaks tempt guests to return often to enjoy his cuisine and fabulous Gulf sunsets.

Flavors From The Sea

Black Cod in Miso

Seafood Risotto

Salmon with Orange Champagne Sauce

Lobster in Papaya Champagne Sauce

Mahi Mahi with Pineapple Confit

Swordfish with Mango Salsa

Pan Seared Snapper

Salmon, Shrimp & Spinach Stack

Grilled Rosemary Shrimp & Pappardelle

Crab Crusted Grouper

Sea Bass, Jap Cha Noodles

Grilled Grouper with Shrimp & Lobster Hash

Braised Wahoo

Panko & Herb Crusted Grouper

Florida Bouillabaisse

Seared Scallops with Mango Slaw

Black Cod in Miso

Serves four

4 skinless cod fillets,
    6 oz each
3/4 cup mirin
3/4 cup sake
1/4 cup sugar
1 tsp finely chopped
    fresh ginger

1/2 cup red miso
peanut oil
4 heads Shanghai bok choy
1 tsp finely chopped fresh ginger
1 tsp chopped garlic
salt & pepper to taste

Combine mirin, sake, sugar and ginger in a pot and bring to a simmer over medium heat for 2 minutes to infuse flavors and burn off the alcohol. Remove from heat, add miso and mix well. Let cool then add cod fillets. Marinate for at least 3 to 4 hours or overnight. Remove from marinade and place under a broiler for 4 to 5 minutes until lightly browned. Or, if you prefer, you may sear the fillets on both sides until lightly browned in peanut oil that well covers the bottom of a saute pan. Finish in a 350° oven for 7 to 8 minutes. Meanwhile, lightly saute the bok choy with the remaining ginger, garlic, salt and pepper in peanut oil until just wilted. Liberally pour the Coconut Milk Sauce over the fish and serve with Shanghai bok choy.

Coconut Milk Sauce

2/3 can coconut milk, 14 oz
5 kaffir lime leaves
2 tblsps mirin
1 tsp Thai Panang curry

Mix all ingredients together well and reduce over medium heat by half, to a sauce consistency.

Note: You can find all of these exotic ingredients in Asian markets or natural food stores.

Seafood Risotto

Serves four

1/2 small onion, 1/4" diced
1-1/2 tblsps olive oil
1/2 tsp chopped garlic
1 cup arborio rice
3/4 cup white wine
2-1/2 cups shrimp stock (page 113)
1 tblsp butter

12 oz clams
12 oz mussels, cleaned
12 large shrimp, peeled & deveined
16 large scallops, abductor muscle removed
12 oz squid, cleaned & thinly sliced
1 cup white wine
1/3 cup Grana Padano cheese, finely grated
1/4 lb baby asparagus spears

Saute onion in olive oil over medium heat until almost translucent. Add garlic, saute briefly and stir in rice. Add 3/4 cup white wine and simmer until the wine is absorbed. Add the shrimp stock in three equal amounts, stirring occasionally, until each is absorbed, until rice is soft but holds shape. After rice is cooked, in a separate pan, lightly saute clams and mussels in butter for 1 to 2 minutes. Add the remaining seafood and saute until the clams and mussels begin to open. Add 1 cup white wine and deglaze the pan. Add the rice and simmer gently until the seafood is cooked, the liquid is absorbed and clams and mussels are open. Once the rice is soft and creamy, stir in the cheese and season to taste. Arrange seafood around rice placed in center of plate and garnish with steamed, crisp tender asparagus.

Salmon with Orange Champagne Sauce

Serves Four

4 salmon fillets, 6 oz each	2 tblsps cracked peppercorns
1 tblsp orange zest, chopped fine	1 tsp kosher salt
1 tblsp chopped fresh parsley	1 medium potato, julienned
1/2 cup olive oil	1 medium sweet potato, julienned
1/4 tsp salt	4 each, baby carrots, broccolini
1 tblsp olive oil	spears, asparagus spears

Create a marinade by combining orange zest, parsley, 1/2 cup olive oil and salt. Dredge the salmon fillets in the marinade then top with kosher salt and peppercorns on top side only. Sear fillets in a teflon or cast iron skillet over very high heat in 1 tablespoon olive oil, peppered side down, for 1 minute to lightly color. Finish in a 400° oven with the peppered side down for 5 minutes. Meanwhile, deep fry julienned potatoes until light brown and crisp (or saute in 2 tblsps olive oil). Serve with steamed carrots, broccolini and asparagus. Drizzle plates with Orange Champagne Sauce and garnish with orange segments.

Orange Champagne Sauce

3 cups orange juice
1 cup champagne (or dry white wine)
2 tblsps chopped shallots
2 cups heavy cream
salt & white pepper to taste

Reduce orange juice, champagne and shallots to a syrup consistency in a stainless steel pan. Add cream and reduce to a sauce consistency. Season to taste.

Serves four

4 Maine lobsters, 1-1/4 to 1-1/2 lbs each
or lobster tails, 4 to 5 oz each
1 tsp butter
3 cups champagne
1 ripe papaya, peeled & seeded
2 tblsps honey
1/2 vanilla bean, split
1-1/2 cups heavy cream
1/2 carrot, julienned
salt & white pepper to taste

Blanch lobster in boiling water for 1-1/2 minutes and remove from water. If using whole lobsters, leave claws to cook for another 6 minutes. Shock tails (and claws) in cold water and pull meat from shells. Saute lobster meat and claw meat in butter until it begins to whiten but not fully cooked. Remove from pan. Finely dice one half of the papaya and slice the other half lengthwise for garnish. Add the champagne to the pan with the diced papaya, honey and vanilla bean. Bring to a boil and reduce to 1/2 cup, close to a syrup consistency. Add the cream and reduce to almost a sauce consistency. Add the carrots and continue to reduce until thickened. Return the lobster to pan, season to taste and cook until lobster is done, focusing more on the tail meat (the claws should be mostly cooked). Serve over sliced papaya with sauce and Spinach Flan (page 111).

Lobster in Papaya Champagne Sauce   Spinach Flan

Mahi Mahi with Pineapple Confit & Dat'l Sweet Pepper Glaze

Serves four

4 mahi mahi fillets, 8 oz each
salt & pepper to taste

Season fillets and grill or sear over medium heat for
4 to 5 minutes on each side. Brush with Dat'l Sweet
Pepper Glaze, top with Pineapple Confit (page 110).

Dat'l Sweet Pepper Glaze
1 roasted red bell pepper (page 56)
2 tblsps Dat'l hot sauce
1 tblsp water
5 sprigs fresh cilantro, chopped
4 tblsps honey
2 tblsps lemon juice
dash cayenne pepper
pinch kosher salt
4 tblsps whole unsalted butter, softened

Peel and seed the pepper, combine with all ingredients except the butter in a food processor. Process
at high speed until thoroughly pureed. Fold into the butter until well incorporated and set aside.

Swordfish with Mango Salsa

Serves four

4 swordfish fillets, 6 oz each,	1 tblsp finely chopped fresh rosemary
skinless & 1" thick	1 tsp chopped fresh thyme
1/8 cup olive oil	1 heaping tblsp chopped fresh basil
1 heaping tsp chopped garlic	

Mix the olive oil with garlic and herbs then brush onto both sides of the fillets. Grill over high heat to make grill marks, reduce heat and cook for 4 to 5 minutes, until cooked in center, turning occasionally. Serve with Mango Salsa.

Mango Salsa

1 medium ripe mango	1/3 cup diced honeydew melon
3 tblsps seasoned rice vinegar	2 tblsps chopped fresh cilantro
1/2 cup olive oil	2 tsps finely diced red pepper
	salt & ground white pepper

Peel and seed the mango then dice one half of the flesh and puree the other half. Add the rice vinegar and olive oil to the pureed mango and mix well. Combine with 1/3 cup diced mango and remaining ingredients. Mix well. Lightly season with salt and ground white pepper to taste. Serve chilled salsa over hot fish.

Pan Seared Snapper
Passion Fruit Beurre Blanc   Balsamic Syrup

Serves four

4 snapper fillets, skinless, 6 to 8 oz each
kosher salt, pepper & paprika to taste
1 tblsp canola oil

Season fillets with salt, pepper and
paprika. Saute in oil, top side down, for
2 minutes or until browned. Carefully
turn and cook for another 2 minutes.
Serve with Passion Fruit Beurre Blanc
and drizzle with Balsamic Syrup.

Passion Fruit Beurre Blanc
6 passion fruits, halved
1 cup white wine
1 cup orange juice
1 tsp chopped garlic
1/2 cup honey
1 cup heavy cream
2 tblsps cornstarch
1/4 lb cold butter, cubed
kosher & crushed red pepper to taste

Balsamic Syrup
1/2 cup balsamic vinegar
3/4 cup sugar

Squeeze the passion fruit into a sauce pan. Whisk in white wine,
orange juice, garlic and honey. Bring to a boil over high heat and
reduce for 2 to 3 minutes. Whisk in the heavy cream and return to
a boil. Ladle out 2 tblsps of the sauce and mix with the cornstarch.
Whisk this cornstarch mixture back into the boiling sauce and
reduce 1 minute until thickened. Strain through a fine mesh sieve.
When fish is almost finished, whisk in butter, a few cubes at a time,
and add pepper. When all of the butter is melted, season with salt.

Stir the sugar into the vinegar in a sauce pan. Bring to a boil
and reduce to a light syrup consistency. Cool before serving.

Serves four

12 oz salmon, dark flesh removed	2 cups white wine
1/3 cup white wine	3 cups heavy cream
salt & pepper to taste	1 lemon, juiced
3 large shallots, minced	1/3 packed cup
1 tblsp butter	chopped fresh dill

Sauce: Saute shallots in butter until soft. Add wine and reduce to a syrup consistency. Add cream and reduce to a sauce consistency. Add lemon juice, finish with dill and heat through when fish is cooked.

Shrimp & Shrimp Mousse

15 oz large shrimp, peeled & deveined
1/3 cup heavy cream

Butterfly 2/3 of the shrimp and set aside. Puree remaining 1/3 of shrimp until very smooth. Add heavy cream and blend to mix well.

Spinach

1/2 lb fresh spinach
1 tblsp olive oil
1/2 tsp chopped garlic
salt & pepper to taste

Briefly blanch spinach in boiling water. Remove and immediately shock in cold water to stop cooking process. Saute with garlic in oil for 1 minute. Season to taste, stir and remove from heat.

Cut salmon into 12 thin slices. Begin making stacks starting with a salmon slice, pipe shrimp mousse on top and season to taste. Place a butterflied shrimp on top followed by a tablespoon of spinach. Repeat this order again, finishing with a salmon slice on top. Splash with wine and tent with foil, careful that the foil does not touch the fish. Bake in a 350° oven for 20 to 30 minutes. Center stacks on plates and pool with sauce.

Grilled Rosemary Shrimp   Fresh Herb Pappardelle

Serves four

12 to 16 large shrimp, peeled & deveined

4 strong rosemary stems, 8" in length

1/4 cup extra virgin olive oil

1 tblsp finely chopped basil

1/2 tsp finely chopped rosemary

salt & pepper to taste

1/2 cup grated Pecorino or Grana Padano cheese

Skewer the shrimp on the rosemary stems with the bottom 3/4 of leaves removed. Create a marinade by mixing the oil, basil and rosemary, then season to taste. Marinate the shrimp for 30 minutes then saute or grill for a few minutes on each side until pink. Serve with Fresh Herb Pappardelle mixed with Pasta Sauce (page 110) and sprinkle with cheese.

Fresh Herb Pappardelle

3 cups semolina flour

2 cups flour

2 tsps salt

1 tblsp finely chopped rosemary

1 tblsp very finely chopped thyme

4 tblsps very finely chopped parsley leaves

3 tblsps olive oil

2 tblsps water

Mix all ingredients with a mixer until dough is smooth and refrigerate for 2 to 3 hours. Roll into sheets through a pasta machine and cut into 1/2" wide ribbons. Boil in salted water until al dente and drain.

Serves four

4 grouper fillets, skinless, 8 oz each
kosher salt & pepper to taste
all purpose flour
1 tblsp canola oil

Season the fillets, dredge lightly in flour and saute in oil, top side down, for 2 minutes or until lightly browned. Transfer to a greased cooking tray. Mold the crab crust over the fish, shaping to the form of the fillets. Bake in a 375° oven for 12 minutes.
Serve with Avery Island Beurre Blanc (page 110).

Crab Crust

1 medium baking potato
canola oil for frying
1/2 lb bacon
1/2 lb lump crabmeat
1/2 cup mayonnaise

2 tblsps chopped fresh cilantro
2 tblsps chopped fresh curly parsley
4 green onions, thinly sliced
1/4 tsp dried thyme
1/4 cup shredded cheddar cheese
kosher salt & pepper to taste

Wash the potato and cut into matchsticks, 1/8" x 1/8" x 1-1/2". Fry in oil until crispy, drain and let cool. Fry the bacon until crispy then crumble. Gently sift through crabmeat, removing any shells. Combine the mayonnaise, bacon, cilantro, parsley, onions, thyme, cheese and crabmeat in a bowl. Using a spatula, fold in the potato matchsticks, mixing thoroughly. Season to taste.

Crab Crusted Grouper   Avery Island Beurre Blanc

Seared Sea Bass Jap Cha Noodles

Serves four

4 sea bass fillets, skin on, 5 oz each

corn oil

salt & pepper to taste

12 oz glass noodles (sweet potato starch noodles)

1 small onion, thinly sliced

1 green pepper, julienned

1 carrot, finely julienned

8 shiitake mushrooms,
    stems removed, thinly sliced
    (or 8 wood ear mushrooms)

1/3 cup corn oil

5 tblsps soy sauce

1 tblsp sesame oil

1-1/4 tsps chili oil

4 tblsps sugar

4 scallions, thinly sliced on a bias

Season fish with salt and pepper to taste. Coat the bottom of a saute pan with corn oil, then sear the fillets over high heat on both sides until lightly browned. Finish in a 350° oven for 5 to 6 minutes.

Cook noodles in boiling, salted water until al dente. Saute onion in 1/4 cup corn oil over medium heat until soft. Add pepper, carrot and mushrooms, then saute until crisp tender. Add soy sauce, sesame oil, chili oil, sugar and mix well. Stir in drained noodles and simmer for a few minutes, allowing the noodles to soak up the flavor. Top with sliced scallions.

Glass noodles and wood ear mushrooms can be found in your local Asian market. If using dried wood ear mushrooms, reconstitute before slicing and adding to the vegetable mixture.

Grilled Grouper Rock Shrimp & Lobster Hash

Serves four
4 grouper fillets, 6 oz each
1/8 cup olive oil
1 heaping tsp chopped garlic

1 tblsp chopped fresh rosemary
1 tsp chopped fresh thyme
1 heaping tblsp chopped fresh basil
salt & pepper to taste

Season fish with salt and pepper. Mix the olive oil with the garlic and herbs. Brush onto both sides of the fillets and grill over high heat on both sides until lightly brown. Finish in a 350° oven for 5 minutes. Serve with Rock Shrimp and Lobster Hash.

Rock Shrimp & Lobster Hash

6 oz rock (or very small) shrimp
6 oz lobster tail meat, diced
1/2 cup olive oil
2 potatoes, peeled & 1/4" cubed
1/2 red pepper, finely chopped
1/2 green pepper, finely chopped

1/2 small red onion, finely chopped
6 scallions, finely chopped
1 tblsp chopped fresh parsley
1/2 cup white wine
1/2 tsp fresh ground black pepper
salt to taste

Fry the potatoes in very hot olive oil over high heat until browned. Remove from pan and set aside. Remove half of the remaining oil then sear the peppers and onion over high heat until caramelized. Add the cooked potatoes and seafood then saute over high heat until the seafood is half cooked. Add scallions, parsley, wine and black pepper. Saute until the wine is absorbed and the seafood is cooked. Season with salt.

Braised Wahoo

Serves four

4 boneless wahoo fillets, 6 oz each
salt & pepper to taste
1/4 cup vegetable oil
5 shiitake mushrooms, sliced
3-1/2 oz enoki mushrooms
1/2 cup clam juice
3/4 cup sherry
5 tblsps soy sauce
1-1/2 cups coconut milk
2 stems lemon grass, 4" each, flattened
pinch of red pepper flakes
4 small kaffir lime leaves
1 tblsp red curry paste

Combine clam juice with remaining ingredients and set aside. Salt and pepper the fillets then sear in vegetable oil in a non-stick pan on one side only until lightly colored. Turn the fillets over then add clam juice mixture and shiitake mushrooms. Bring to a simmer and braise for 4 to 6 minutes until sauce is slightly reduced. Remove the fillets and discard lemon grass. Cut the end off the enoki mushrooms and separate. Add to the sauce with pepper to taste. Simmer for 2 minutes then return fillets to the sauce and heat just until flavors are blended. Serve in sauce with sauteed bok choy and steamed basmati rice.

Serves four

4 skinless grouper fillets, 4 to 5 oz each	3 cups panko bread crumbs
salt & pepper to taste	3 heaping tblsps each, finely chopped fresh chives, fresh parsley, fresh dill, fresh tarragon
flour for dusting	
2 eggs, beaten	1/3 cup olive oil

Combine bread crumbs with chopped herbs in a bowl and mix well. Season fillets with salt and pepper, dust with flour then dredge in beaten eggs. Coat with the bread crumb and herb mixture, shaking off excess crumbs. Saute in olive oil on both sides until well browned. If necessary, finish in a 300° oven for 5 to 6 minutes, or until an internal temperature of 145° is reached. Serve with Red Pepper Aioli.

Red Pepper Aioli
1 small red pepper
2 egg yolks
1 tsp water
1-1/2 cups olive oil
1/2 tsp finely chopped garlic
1 lemon, juiced
salt & fresh pepper to taste

Thoroughly coat the pepper with olive oil and sear in a small saute pan until brown on all sides. Remove to a plate, cover with plastic wrap and let steam. When cooled, remove skin and seeds then finely dice the flesh. Set aside.

Whip egg yolks with water in a mixing bowl over low heat until yolks are warm and frothy. Whip in a few drops of olive oil then slowly drizzle in remaining oil while continuously whipping. You should have a thick mayonnaise. Remove from heat, add garlic, lemon juice and diced pepper. Season to taste.

Panko & Herb Crusted Grouper Red Pepper Aioli

Florida Bouillabaisse

For The Broth:
2-1/4 lbs white fish bones
2 tblsps olive oil
1/2 medium onion, sliced
1 celery stalk, sliced
2 cups white wine
2 cups water
1/4 tsp black pepper
2 tblsps chopped garlic
1 tblsp chopped shallot
1 carrot, finely chopped
1/4 onion, finely chopped
1/4 cup Pernod
2 tblsps tomato paste
2 tblsps finely diced pepper
1 healthy pinch saffron (1/2 gram)

3/4 lb grouper, cut into 1-1/2" chunks
3/4 lb mahi mahi, cut into 1-1/2" chunks
1/2 lb lobster tail in shell, cut into chunks
1/2 lb shrimp, peeled & deveined
3/4 lb scallops, muscle removed
salt & pepper to taste
Seafood Risotto (page 32)

Serves Four

The success of this dish depends on the broth. It is well worth the time it takes to slowly simmer the rich flavors.

Lightly saute sliced onion and celery in 1 tablespoon olive oil. Add wine, water and fish bones. Season with black pepper and simmer for 25 minutes, careful not to boil. Strain broth. Saute garlic, shallot, chopped carrot and onion in remaining olive oil. Add Pernod, tomato paste and strained broth, then simmer for 25 minutes until carrots are tender. Puree, return to heat then add pepper and saffron. Simmer for 10 minutes to bring out the saffron color. Add all of the seafood to the broth and simmer for 8 to 10 minutes until seafood is cooked. Season to taste with salt and pepper.
Pour bouillabaisse around risotto placed in center of bowls. Serve with extra broth and thinly sliced grilled garlic bread.

Seared Scallops Mango Slaw Cilantro Pesto

Serves four

1-1/2 to 2 lbs very large scallops, abductor muscles removed
olive oil
kosher salt & black pepper to taste

Lightly coat scallops with olive oil and season to taste. Coat the bottom of a cast iron skillet or a heavy bottomed pan with olive oil. Heat oil until very hot and almost smoking. Sear the scallops on one side until browned then turn and brown other side. (Be careful not to overload your pan. This results in boiling instead of searing.) Serve with Mango Slaw and Cilantro Pesto.

Mango Slaw
1/2 mango, julienned
1/2 carrot, julienned
1/4 red onion, julienned
1 packed cup julienned cabbage

1/3 jalapeno pepper, seeded, chopped fine
4 tblsps rice vinegar
1 heaping tblsp mayonnaise
2 tblsps minced fresh mint
salt & pepper to taste

Mix the vegetables together. Combine the vinegar and mayonnaise and blend into vegetables. Sprinkle with mint, season to taste and stir well.

Cilantro Pesto
1 cup cilantro leaves
2/3 cup olive oil

1/4 cup walnut pieces
1/4 cup pine nuts
salt & pepper to taste

Combine all ingredients in a blender and pulse to a smooth pesto consistency.

Fun, sun, paddleboats and pirates...what more could you ask for in a family vacation? At TradeWinds, families find time to reconnect, kids make new friends from all over the world, and treasured memories are made to be savored for years to come.

Overlooking the Gulf of Mexico, TradeWinds Island Resorts provide limitless beachfront recreation and activities, from wave runners and parasailing to kite flying and castle building. Families also cruise along our meandering waterway on paddleboats.

RedBeard the Pirate brings his original songs of the seas and tall tales to regale the young and young at heart at TradeWinds Island Grand. Supervised activities, crafts and camaraderie abound, where kids are never bored and the grown-ups can find a little time for their own pleasure and relaxation.

Flavors From Ashore

Rack of Lamb

Roquefort Stuffed Tenderloin

Grilled Stuffed Veal Chop

Jerk Pork Tenderloin

Simple Braised Short Ribs

Korean Barbecue Brochettes

New York Strip Steak

Cumin Dusted Chicken Breasts

Potato Gnocchi

Turkey Saltimbocca

Grilled Pork Chops

Lamb Sheherezade

Chicken Breasts, Gorgonzola & Portobello

Rack Of Lamb

Black-Eyed Pea Ragout, Fig & Port Sauce

Black-Eyed Pea Ragout

Serves Four

2 cups black-eyed peas
1 tblsp salt
water
1/4 cup olive oil
1 cup diced onion
1 cup diced red pepper
1/2 cup diced carrot

1 cup diced zucchini (skin only)
1 cup diced summer squash (skin only)
1 tblsp chopped garlic
1 tblsp finely chopped fresh rosemary
1 cup red wine
1-1/2 cups demi glace (page 111)
salt & fresh ground black pepper to taste

Blanch peas in salted water to cover 4 to 6 minutes on a light boil until tender. Dice all vegetables into 1/4" squares. Heat oil in a saute pan until very hot so that the vegetables will caramelize during cooking. Saute onions until lightly caramelized, then remove from pan. Saute red pepper and carrots until just tender and browned, then remove from pan. Saute the zucchini and squash until just tender. Return the onions, pepper and carrots to the pan and add garlic, rosemary and wine. Over medium heat, reduce until almost dry, add demi glace and season with black pepper. Drain peas, add to mixture and mix well. Reduce until ragout is slightly thickened then season with salt and pepper to taste.

Rack Of Lamb

2 racks of lamb, 8 bones
   each, bones cleaned
1 tblsp olive oil
salt & pepper

Coat the bottom of a saute pan with olive oil and heat until very hot. Halve the lamb racks then liberally salt and pepper all sides. Saute on both sides until lightly seared. Finish in a 350° oven for 15 to 18 minutes to an internal temperature of 136° to 138°. Let rest for 15 minutes before slicing. Serve with Black-Eyed Pea Ragout and Fig and Port Sauce. Garnish with sliced figs and grilled fennel.

Fig & Port Sauce

1 large shallot, chopped fine
1/2 tsp olive oil
1/2 cup demi glace (page 111)
4 brown Turkey figs, diced
1/4 cup port

Saute shallots in olive oil, add demi glace and reduce slightly. Add the figs and reduce over medium heat to a sauce consistency and until the figs begin to break apart. Stir in the port. Note: If using dried figs, reduce the amount used by one third.

Roquefort Stuffed Tenderloin

Serves Four

4 beef tenderloins, 6 to 8 oz each   olive oil
2 oz Roquefort cheese   salt & pepper to taste

Cut a small slit in the side of each tenderloin. Run a knife from the slit to the left and to the right, making a pocket.
Stuff each pocket with 1/2 oz cheese and squeeze shut. Salt and pepper to taste and sear in very hot olive oil on
each side until lightly browned. Remove from heat, cover the top of each tenderloin with duxelle and sprinkle with
bread crumbs. Finish in a 350° oven for 12 minutes, to an internal temperature of 130°. Remove and serve.

Duxelle

1/2 lb mushrooms, finely chopped   2 tblsps butter, melted   1/4 cup heavy cream
1/4 lb smoked ham, 1/8" diced   1/4 cup white wine   1/2 cup bread crumbs
1 tblsp finely chopped shallot   1/2 tsp chopped tarragon   salt & black pepper to taste

Saute the mushrooms, ham and shallots in butter
over medium heat for 2 minutes. Add the wine
and tarragon and reduce until dry. Add the heavy
cream and reduce again until dry, to a paste
consistency. Season to taste.

Grilled Stuffed Veal Chop Potato Pancakes

Serves four

4 veal (or pork) chops, 10 to 12 oz each
1 small onion, diced
2 tblsps olive oil
2 tsps chopped garlic
3 oz sliced shiitake mushrooms
1 tblsp chopped fresh tarragon
6 oz smoked mozzarella cheese, sliced
salt & pepper to taste
1/2 cup demi glace (page 111)

Saute diced onion in oil until caramelized. Add garlic, mushrooms and tarragon then saute until mushrooms are cooked through. Season to taste. Trim and clean the chops, then clean the bones. Using a sharp knife, make an incision starting close to the bone of the chops and cut 2 inches through the middle, creating a wide pocket. Stuff the chops with the mushroom mixture, insert cheese, then pinch shut. Lightly coat with oil, season with salt and pepper then sear on both sides until browned. Finish cooking in a 325° oven for 10 to 15 minutes. Drizzle with demi glace and serve with Potato Pancakes (page 113).

Jerk Pork Tenderloin   Grilled Pineapple Relish   Serves six

Jerk Marinade

3 tblsps ground allspice	2 garlic cloves, minced
1 tsp ground cinnamon	1/4 cup red wine
1/2 tsp freshly grated nutmeg	1/4 cup vegetable oil
1 tblsp ground coriander	ground chili pepper to taste
4 scallions, finely chopped	salt & fresh ground black pepper

Mix all ingredients together into a paste. Spread over entire meat surface. Allow meat to marinate for 6 to 8 hours, then remove from marinade before cooking.

1-1/2 lb pork tenderloin	4 ripe plantains
olive oil	cooked black beans & rice

Trim tenderloin of fat and silver skin then marinate. Generously coat the bottom of an oven proof skillet, preferably cast iron, with oil. Heat oil until very hot and sear the loin on all sides until almost blackened. Finish in a 350° oven for 20 to 25 minutes, to an internal temperature of 140° to 145°. Remove from oven and let rest 5 to 10 minutes before slicing. Meanwhile, cut the plantains into 1/2 inch slices and saute in oil until light brown. Serve with Grilled Pineapple Relish (page 113), black beans and rice.

Simple Braised Short Ribs Jardiniere

Serves six to eight

5 lbs beef short ribs
flour
salt & pepper to taste
vegetable oil
2 cans beef broth, 10.5 oz each
2 cans petite diced tomatoes, 14.5 oz each
1/2 cup brown sugar
2 cups red wine

1 tblsp chopped garlic
3 sprigs fresh thyme
2 cups water
1 carrot
2 celery stalks
1 red pepper
1 cup cooked green peas

Lightly dust ribs with flour and season with salt and pepper. Cover the bottom of a heavy pot with oil and sear ribs until browned on all sides. Add broth, tomatoes, brown sugar, wine, garlic, thyme and water. Cover tightly, bring to a simmer and braise for 45 minutes. Uncover and braise for another 45 minutes until the meat is very tender and falling off the bones. Slice the carrot, celery and pepper into strips 1-1/2 inches by 1/4 inch. Add to the pot and cook for 10 minutes. Serve ribs with sauce, garlic mashed potatoes and garnish with green peas.

I just had to add this recipe because I love braised short ribs. They are simply the best, and easiest, comfort food!

Korean Barbecue Brochettes

Serves Four

2 lbs trimmed sirloin (or any tender beef)
steamed jasmine rice
4 scallions, finely chopped

1 tblsp soy sauce
1 tsp sesame oil
1-1/2 tblsps ginger

1 tblsp sugar
2 tblsps sherry

Create a marinade by combining the scallions with the remaining ingredients. Cut the beef into 1-1/2 to 2 inch chunks. Marinate for at least 2 hours. Remove from marinade, place on skewers and grill or saute for 3 to 4 minutes on each side over high heat. Serve with rice and Stir Fry Vegetables.

Stir Fry Vegetables

2 tblsps soy sauce
2 tsps sesame oil
2 tsps sesame seeds
3 tsps sherry
2 tsps Nam Pla (fish sauce)
1 tblsp honey

6 shiitake mushrooms, sliced
1/2 cabbage, sliced
2 cups broccoli flowerets
1 red pepper, diced
1 tblsp oil
1/2 tsp chopped fresh ginger
2 tblsps water

Mix the soy sauce with the next five ingredients and set aside. Saute the vegetables in oil until crisp tender. Add the ginger, water and the reserved sauce and saute until heated through.

New York Strip Steak Red Stripe Mustard Gravy

Serves four

4 sirloin strip steaks, 12 oz each
salt & pepper to taste

Red Stripe Mustard Gravy
1 cup demi glace (page 111)
1/2 cup Red Stripe beer
1/4 cup honey
2 heaping tblsps brown mustard
2 tblsps cornstarch
kosher salt and pepper to taste

Whisk the demi glace and beer together in a sauce pan and bring to a boil. Whisk in the honey and mustard then return to a boil. Ladle out 2 tablespoons of the boiling liquid and stir into the cornstarch. Whisk this cornstarch mixture until smooth, return to boiling sauce, reduce heat and simmer for 15 minutes until sauce consistency. Season to taste.
This gravy is also great with chicken or pork.

Salt and pepper steaks and grill over high heat for 4 minutes on each side for medium rare. Serve with Red Stripe Mustard Gravy.

Bermudas is the casual restaurant at Island Grand; famous for its aged steaks, fresh seafood and fabled Gulf Coast sunsets.

Serves four

Bacon & Corn Galettes

3 strips bacon, diced

1 small onion, 1/4" diced

3 cups fresh or thawed corn kernels

1/4 cup diced onion

1 egg

1/4 cup milk

3/4 cup flour

2 tsps baking powder

salt & fresh black pepper to taste

6 small ramekins (3 oz), well buttered

Saute bacon until crispy. Add onions and cook over medium heat until translucent. Set aside. Puree half of the corn kernels in a blender or food processor, adding a little water if too thick. In a mixing bowl, combine pureed corn, the bacon onion mixture and all remaining ingredients. Mix well and season to taste. Place in ramekins and bake in a 350° oven for approximately 20 minutes, until cooked in the center.

4 boneless chicken breasts, cleaned,
   wing bone in, 4 oz each

2 tblsps olive oil

1 tblsp cumin

1 tblsp finely chopped fresh cilantro

salt & pepper to taste

Briefly marinate chicken breasts in olive oil, cumin, cilantro, salt and pepper. Remove from marinade and sear in a hot saute pan until lightly browned on both sides. Finish in a 350° oven for 15 to 18 minutes, until an internal temperature of 155° is reached. Remove from oven and serve whole with Bacon and Corn Galettes (or, if desired, let rest 5 minutes before slicing). Drizzle with a good, aged balsamic vinegar.

Cumin Dusted Chicken Breasts Bacon & Corn Galettes

Potato Gnocchi Wild Mushrooms

Serves four

1-3/4 lbs potatoes (3 large potatoes)   2 eggs
2-1/4 cups all purpose flour   salt to taste

Boil the potatoes, then peel and mash. Place in a bowl with the flour, add the eggs then season with salt. Knead in the bowl then transfer to a board and continue to knead until the dough is soft, elastic and smooth. Form into rolls 1 inch in diameter and cut into segments about 3/4 inch long. Press each segment against the back of a fork with your finger to make ridges and a small indentation. Boil in salted water until they float to the surface and for about 1 minute longer. Drain, mix with Wild Mushrooms.

Wild Mushrooms

1 tblsp finely chopped shallots
1-1/2 tblsps finely chopped garlic
1/4 cup olive oil
1 cup white wine

1 to 1-1/4 lbs assorted sliced mushrooms
(portobello, shiitake, porcini, cremini, domestic white)
1-1/2 cups heavy cream
3/4 cup green peas
salt & pepper to taste

Saute shallots and garlic in olive oil for 2 to 3 minutes over low heat. Add white wine and mushrooms then simmer over high heat for 3 to 4 minutes. Add cream, return to a simmer, then add peas and cooked gnocchi. Season to taste and simmer for a few minutes to thicken and to blend flavors.

Turkey Saltimbocca

This is a tasty variation of traditional saltimbocca which is made with veal. Prosciutto, ham that has been salt-cured, is always used. Saltimbocca means "jump mouth", for strong flavors.

Serves four

1-1/2 lbs turkey breast,
   cut into 8 thin slices
5 to 6 fresh sage leaves
8 thin slices prosciutto
8 thin slices provolone cheese
flour
2 tblsps olive oil
2 large portobello mushrooms, sliced
1/2 cup marsala wine
1/2 cup demi glace (page 111)
1/2 cup chicken stock or water
2 heaping tblsps butter
salt & pepper to taste

Pound the turkey slices with a meat mallet until flat. Remove stems from sage leaves and mince. Sprinkle turkey slices with sage, top with cheese followed with prosciutto. Roll up tightly and flatten with a quick tap of the meat mallet. Season and dredge in flour, shaking off excess. Saute in very hot oil, seamed side down first, for 1 to 2 minutes on each side until browned. Add mushrooms, wine, demi glace and chicken stock. Simmer for 3 to 4 minutes, then remove turkey. Reduce sauce until thick, then add butter. Season to taste and simmer for 1 to 2 minutes. Drizzle turkey with sauce and serve with Sauteed Spinach (page 112) and a side of pesto pasta, if desired.

Grilled Pork Chops   Apple, Onion Pomegranate Relish

Serves four

sugar

4 thick pork chops, 10 to 12 oz each

1/2 cup pomegranate juice

salt & pepper

3 tblsps vegetable oil

Lightly dust chops with salt, pepper and sugar. Marinate in pomegranate juice and oil for 20 minutes. Remove from marinade and grill over hickory chips until an internal temperature of 145° to 150° is reached. Serve with Apple, Onion Pomegranate Relish, Baked Red Potatoes and sauteed broccoli. raab, if desired.

Apple, Onion Pomegranate Relish

1/4 cup vegetable oil

2 sprigs thyme, leaves minced

1-1/2 onions, sliced 1/4" thick

pinch crushed red pepper

3/4 cup pomegranate juice

pinch black pepper

2 apples, peeled, seeded & sliced

1/4 cup pomegranate seeds

4 tblsps demi glace (page 111)

1/4 cup chopped mint

Saute onions in oil until caramelized. Add pomegranate juice and cook for 1 minute. Add apples, demi glace, thyme, red and black pepper then cook down until dry. Add pomegranate seeds and mint, then cook until heated through.

Baked Red Potatoes

1 lb small red potatoes   1 tsp garlic

1/4 cup olive oil   salt & pepper to taste

In a bowl, toss potatoes with oil, garlic and season to taste. Bake at 350° for 25 minutes, depending on size, until cooked through.

Serves four

2 racks of lamb, cut into 16 chops	1/3 to 1/2 cup chopped mango
salt & pepper to taste	1 tblsp chopped red pepper
2 tblsps olive oil	2 tblsps chopped fresh cilantro
1 jar mango chutney, 9 oz	1/4 cup chopped peanuts

Clean bones of chops, salt and pepper lamb chops then quickly sear in olive oil for 1 minute on each side. Mix the chutney with the mango, pepper and cilantro. Top each chop with a teaspoon of this mixture and sprinkle with peanuts. Finish in a 350° oven for 9 to 10 minutes. Drizzle with demi glace (page 111), serve with Eggplant Saute and Anna Potatoes (page 112).

Eggplant Saute

1 medium eggplant	1/2 red pepper, 1" diced
1/4 cup olive oil	1 tblsp chopped garlic
1/2 onion, 1" diced	1 cup white wine
1/2 green pepper, 1" diced	2 tblsps chopped fresh basil

Peel the eggplant, leaving skin on about 1/4 of it, then dice into 1" squares. Saute in oil until lightly browned and softened, then add the onion, pepper and garlic. Saute for 1 to 2 minutes, adding no more oil even if mixture becomes dry. Add basil and wine and gently deglaze until eggplant is cooked. Add water if necessary. Season with salt and pepper to taste.

Lamb Sheherezade

Chicken Breasts Stuffed with Gorgonzola & Portobello

Serves four

4 skinless chicken breasts, cleaned, wing bone in
2 oz gorgonzola cheese
1 large portobello mushroom
olive oil
4 large basil leaves, julienned
salt & pepper to taste

Trim excess fat from breasts. Starting from the wing bone, cut a pocket on the upper side of the breasts straight back. Repeat, cutting on the lower side of the breasts, creating an oval pocket. Remove the stem and gills from the portobello. Slice, salt and pepper, then saute in olive oil until wilted. Place 1/2 oz cheese in the breast pockets, followed by several mushroom slices and a small amount of basil. Pinch the pocket closed, rub with olive oil, season and sprinkle with remaining basil. Sear in an oven proof pan in olive oil, skin side down, until browned. Turn breasts over and finish in a 350° oven for 15 to 20 minutes, until 155° near the leg joint. Serve with Red Pepper Polenta and Pan Gravy (page 112).

Red Pepper Polenta
1/2 roasted red pepper (page 56)
1 cup slightly ground corn meal
2-1/4 cups chicken stock or water
1 tsp salt
1/2 to 3/4 oz butter

Skin, seed and dice pepper into 1/4" pieces. In a large pot, bring salted stock to a boil. Add corn meal slowly, keeping stock at a boil, stirring constantly with a wooden spoon. Stir and cook for 20 minutes. Add butter and pepper and stir for 5 to 10 minutes more until the polenta begins to peel from the sides of the pot. Remove from heat and serve immediately.

If love and romance are on your menu, TradeWinds Island Resorts combine all the ingredients to create the idyllic setting for weddings, honeymoons, anniversaries or just a very nice surprise getaway for two.

The friendly and award-winning TradeWinds staff cater to your every need and our culinary professionals create the perfect menus for your wedding or private celebration. Romance rooms and honeymoon suites beckon, red wine facials and aromatherapy massages tempt your senses, and the gentle hush of a sea breeze lulls you into relaxation in a seaside hammock.

Sweet Flavors

Raspberry Almond Tart

Orange, Kiwi & Strawberry Napoleon

Poached Pears

Flourless Chocolate Torte

Key Lime Cheesecake

White Chocolate Mousse & Raspberry Stack

Banana Creme Brulee

Raspberry Almond Tart

Makes one 11" tart

Tart dough
Almond filling
1 jar raspberry preserves, 14 oz
2-1/2 oz sliced raw almonds

Tart Dough

1/2 cup sugar
13 oz butter
1 egg
1 tsp vanilla
3-1/2 cups flour

Mix sugar, butter, egg and vanilla at low speed until well combined. Add flour and mix only until dough is smooth. Place dough on a paper lined pan and refrigerate for 30 minutes. Note: This recipe makes enough dough for 2 tarts. We suggest you freeze one for easy use at another time.

Almond Filling

2 cans almond paste, 8 oz each
6 tblsps sugar
7 oz unsalted butter, softened
1-1/4 cups beaten eggs

Place almond paste and sugar in a mixing bowl. Gradually add softened butter while mixing at low speed. After all butter has been incorporated and mix is smooth, add eggs a bit at a time, scraping bowl occasionally for full incorporation.

On a floured surface, roll out the tart dough until it is large enough to fill the bottom and sides of an 11 inch tart pan. Spread the raspberry preserves evenly across the bottom. Using a pastry bag, pipe almond filling in a spiral motion, starting in the center and working your way to the outside. This will insure that the preserves stay evenly spread. Smooth the top of the tart with a spatula and sprinkle with sliced almonds. Bake at 325° for 10 to 15 minutes until browned. Serve warm or cold.

Serves ten   Makes 2 stacks, 3" x 10"

1 box puff pastry sheets
4 oranges, peeled & sliced
6 kiwis, peeled & sliced
10 strawberries, fanned
confectioners' sugar for dusting

Cut pastry sheets into thirds lengthwise. Liberally prick with a fork to control the rise of the pastry while baking. Bake at 425° for 10 to 15 minutes until lightly browned and fully cooked.

Pastry Cream
1 pint milk
1/2 vanilla bean, split
6 tblsps cornstarch
4 oz sugar
1/4 tsp salt
1 whole egg
3 egg yolks
1 tblsp Grand Marnier

Combine milk and vanilla in a heavy bottomed saucepan and bring to a boil, being careful not to burn. Meanwhile, mix the cornstarch, sugar and salt in a bowl. Gradually whisk the egg and egg yolks into the sugar mixture until smooth. Slowly add scalded milk, continually whipping. When well combined, return this mixture to the saucepan and whisk over medium heat until it begins to boil and thicken. Stir in the Grand Marnier, remove from heat and pour into a shallow pan. Cover with plastic, let cool.

Begin building the dessert by spreading cooled pastry cream on the bottom pastry then layer with kiwi slices. Cover this with another layer of pastry, spread with pastry cream then layer with orange slices. Top with last layer of pastry and dust with confectioners' sugar. Cut into desired serving sizes and garnish with a fanned strawberry. Serve immediately or refrigerate and serve within 3 hours.

Orange, Kiwi & Strawberry Napoleon

Poached Pears

4 semi-ripe pears, Bosc or Bartlett	1/4 cinnamon stick
4 cups burgundy wine	2 Granny Smith apples
1-1/4 cups sugar	8 oz mascarpone cheese

Combine wine, sugar and cinnamon in a pot and bring to a simmer. Peel and add pears, making sure that they are completely covered, and gently simmer for 20 minutes or until softened. If apples are desired, peel and cut them into barrel shapes then add them to the pot and simmer for the last 10 minutes. Remove from heat and let the fruit cool in the syrup to absorb color.

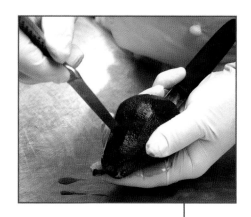

Remove the pears from the syrup and core them by first cutting a small slit near the top with a paring knife, severing the core. Cut through the bottom of the pear with an apple corer to remove the core. Pipe the mascarpone cheese into the pears. Reduce the syrup by half over medium heat to a sauce consistency. Place pears on plates, fan apples if included, and drizzle plates with sauce. Finish with orange segments.

Flourless Chocolate Torte

8 oz semisweet chocolate, chopped

1-1/2 sticks unsalted butter, softened

3/4 cup sugar

7 eggs, separated, at room temperature

1-1/2 cups ground pecans

flour for dusting

2 cups Chocolate Ganache (page 112)

Serves twelve

Garnish

1 cup finely chopped pecans

1-1/2 cups powdered sugar

1 egg yolk

3 to 4 drops lemon juice

Preheat oven to 350°. Line the bottom of a 10 inch springform pan with wax paper. Butter the paper and pan sides and thoroughly dust with flour. Tap pan to remove and discard excess flour.

Melt chocolate in top of double boiler over simmering water until smooth. Remove from heat and cool slightly. In a separate bowl, cream butter and sugar together. Add egg yolks, one at a time, blending well after each. Beat in melted chocolate and ground pecans.

In a separate bowl, beat egg whites until stiff and glossy. Gently fold into chocolate mixture, combining well. Pour into springform pan and smooth with a spatula. Bake for 40 to 50 minutes, until crust begins to form and top puffs, careful not to overcook. Remove and cool for 15 minutes. Invert onto wire rack. When thoroughly cooled, peel off paper and move to a platter. Spread warm Chocolate Ganache over top and sides. Garnish by pressing chopped nuts into sides. In a bowl, combine powdered sugar, egg yolk and lemon juice. Stir until smooth, then pipe through a narrow lipped pastry bag in a spiral pattern on top. Make a "X" by dragging a thin bladed knife from the center of the spiral to outside edges. Drag the knife in the opposite direction between each line. Cool, slice and serve with fresh fruit and mango puree, if desired.

Serves twelve

1-1/2 cups finely ground Graham cracker crumbs
2 tblsps sugar
2 tblsps melted butter
2 tblsps corn syrup
Make a crust by mixing the Graham cracker crumbs with sugar, melted butter and corn syrup. Lightly butter sides of springform pan and press mixture firmly into the bottom. Bake at 350° for 5 to 8 minutes. Let cool completely.

Cream Cheese Mixture

2-1/2 lbs cream cheese, softened	4 tblsps flour
	6 eggs
1-1/2 cups sugar	1-1/2 cups Key lime juice
2 cups sour cream	1 tsp vanilla

Blend cream cheese with sugar until smooth. Add sour cream in thirds, scraping the sides of the bowl, blending smoothly with absolutely no lumps. Add the eggs, lime juice and vanilla. Thoroughly incorporate and pour over crust in springform pan. Evenly distribute and smooth top with a spatula. Bake in a 325° oven for 1 hour until the top just begins to turn light brown and center is firm. Cool completely before removing from pan. Garnish with whipped cream and Key lime slices.

Key Lime Cheesecake

White Chocolate Mousse & Raspberry Stack

Serves ten

30 tuiles

White chocolate mousse (must be made 1 day ahead)

1 pint fresh raspberries

White Chocolate Mousse

12 oz white chocolate

6 oz butter

5 eggs, separated

1 tblsp Grand Marnier

7 tblsps sugar

Melt chocolate and butter in a pan. In a mixing bowl, beat egg yolks and Grand Marnier until thick and creamy, then set aside. In a separate bowl, whip egg whites until peaks begin to form. Add sugar and continue to whip into glossy, stiff peaks. Fold the egg yolk and Grand Marnier mixture into the chocolate and butter mixture. Then, fold the egg whites into this mixture in three equal amounts. Refrigerate overnight.

Tuiles

1 tblsp salted butter

1/3 cup confectioners' sugar

1/2 cup sliced almonds

2 tblsps flour

1/4 cup egg whites

1/8 tsp salt

Preheat oven to 400°. Melt butter over low heat and pour into a mixing bowl. Add sugar, almonds, flour, egg whites, salt and gently fold to combine. Spoon 1 teaspoon of batter onto a nonstick cookie sheet, using a fork to spread into a 2 inch circle (dip fork in water between pressings to avoid sticking). Bake cookies 3 to 5 minutes until light brown on edges. Using a thin metal spatula, immediately remove from pan onto a level surface to cool. Return to oven briefly if cookies tend to stick. Let cool and cover to keep cookies crisp.

Place 3 to 4 raspberries on a tuile and <u>gently</u> spoon in enough mousse to fill center. Repeat process, top with a tuile and garnish with a raspberry. Gently lift with a spatula onto plates and serve <u>immediately</u>.

Banana Creme Brulee

Serves five

1 vanilla bean
1-1/4 cups heavy cream
2 tblsps sugar
3 egg yolks

Scrape the vanilla bean into 1-1/4 cups heavy cream and bring to a scald. Meanwhile, whip the 2 tablespoons of sugar and egg yolks over low heat until yolks are warmed and begin to froth. Slowly add to the scalded vanilla cream.

3 tblsps sugar
1/3 cup milk
1/3 cup heavy cream
2 whole eggs
5 ramekins

In a separate bowl, mix 3 tablespoons sugar with the milk and heavy cream, then add the whole eggs, stirring to thoroughly combine. Slowly add scalded cream mixture, whipping to prevent separation. Press through a cheesecloth. Pour into ramekins (or fluted ceramic bowls) and bake in a 1/4 inch water bath in a 325° oven for 15 to 20 minutes until the custard has set. Remove and refrigerate.

1 to 2 bananas
1 cup sugar

Thinly slice the bananas and arrange over cooled custards. Liberally sprinkle with sugar and caramelize with a propane torch.

Additonal Flavors

Pineapple Confit

1/2 fresh pineapple, peeled & 1/2" diced
1/4 red onion, thinly sliced
1-1/2 cups melted butter
1/2 sprig fresh rosemary
1 tblsp chopped fresh cilantro
kosher salt & pepper to taste

Combine the pineapple, onion and butter in a saucepan, then add the rosemary sprig. Bring to a boil and immediately reduce to a very low simmer. Cover and continue to simmer for 30 minutes. Remove from heat and leave covered for 30 minutes more. Remove the rosemary and drain excess liquid, reserving the pineapple and onion confit. Before serving, saute the confit over high heat until the pineapple and onion are golden brown. Add the cilantro and season to taste.

Herb Pappardelle Pasta Sauce

1 onion, thinly sliced
1 red pepper, julienned
2 tblsps chopped garlic
3/4 cup olive oil
3 artichoke hearts, cooked & cleaned
   (or 8 oz canned & quartered)
1/8 cup aged balsamic vinegar
salt & pepper to taste

Saute onion, pepper and garlic in olive oil until just tender. Add artichokes and vinegar then heat through. Season to taste and mix with pasta.

Avery Island Beurre Blanc

3 packed tblsps cornstarch
2 tblsps water
7 tblsps tabasco sauce
1/2 cup white wine
2 tblsps fresh lemon juice
1/4 cup water
1-1/4 cups heavy cream
4 tblsps unsalted cold butter, cubed
kosher salt to taste

Mix the cornstarch with 2 tablespoons water until smooth and set aside. Combine the tabasco sauce, wine, lemon juice and 1/4 cup water in a saucepan. Bring to a boil and whisk in the heavy cream. Return to a boil, whisk in the cornstarch mixture and reduce to a low simmer for 3 minutes. Remove from heat, whisk in the butter a few cubes at a time. When all butter is melted, season with salt to taste.

Spinach Flan

1 tblsp butter (as needed)

5 oz fresh spinach, stemmed

1/2 tblsp chopped garlic

1 egg

1/3 cup heavy cream

salt & pepper to taste

4 small ramekins, 3 oz each

Blanch spinach in boiling water for 1 minute. Remove and shock in cold water then squeeze out excess water. Chop in a food processor. Add garlic, egg, cream and season to taste. Pulse to combine then pour into 4 small ramekins that have been well buttered. Bake in a water bath at 350° for 25 to 30 minutes until firm in the center. Cool slightly before inverting onto plate.

Demi Glace   (Makes 2 quarts)

Although this sauce takes a good deal of time to make, it is easy and well worth it. It is an essential for all professional chefs. The flavor created through the reduction of natural gelatins can make the difference between a good meal and a fantastic meal. Mix with any wine and reduce to a sauce consistency. (Demi glace can be frozen. Freeze in ice trays for easy measurement.)

2-1/2 lbs oxtail bones

4-1/2 lbs beef bones

4 lbs veal bones

vegetable oil

3 medium onions, rough chopped

3 carrots, rough chopped

4 celery stalks, rough chopped

5 oz tomato paste

1/2 bottle red wine

2-1/2 gallons water

Generously coat bones with oil and roast in a roasting pan for 35 to 40 minutes in a 350° oven. Turn bones, add vegetables and roast for another 30 minutes until bones are light brown and vegetables are caramelized. Be careful that neither are roasted until black because it will make your sauce bitter. Move bones and vegetables to a canning pot and add tomato paste, wine and water. Bring to a simmer, being careful not to boil or broth will become cloudy. Cover and simmer for 48 hours. Remove the bones, strain through cheesecloth and return to heat. Bring to a light boil and reduce to 2 quarts, skimming the fat and skin from the top often.

Dipping Sauce for Pot Stickers

1/4 cup rice vinegar
3 tblsps honey
3 tblsps soy sauce
1-1/2 tsps chili oil

2 tblsps grated carrots
1 tblsp sesame seeds
1 scallion, thinly sliced

Combine all ingredients and mix well.

Chocolate Ganache

1 cup whipping cream
10 oz semisweet chocolate, chopped
1 to 2 tblsps Grand Marnier

Scald cream in a sauce pan to just below boiling. Remove from heat and gently stir in chocolate until thoroughly melted. Stir in Grand Marnier and cool to room temperature.

Anna Potatoes

2 large baking potatoes
salt & white pepper to taste
vegetable oil

Slice potatoes very thinly, pat dry then divide into four stacks. Do not rinse. Spread into fan shapes. Generously coat the bottom of a heavy saute pan with oil and press fans into pan. Avoid getting oil between slices. Fry over medium high heat until edges are browned. Gently flip and fry until the other side is browned. Rearrange slices into fan shapes before serving if they separate.

Chicken Pan Gravy

1/2 cup white wine
3 tblsps demi glace (page 111)
1 oz cold butter
salt & pepper to taste

Using the same pan, with drippings, that you seared the breasts in, add wine and demi glace over medium heat and reduce to sauce consistency. Whip in butter, season and whisk until butter emulsifies.

Sauteed Spinach

1 lb fresh spinach
1 tblsp butter
1 tblsp olive oil
1 tsp chopped garlic
salt & pepper to taste

Remove stems from spinach, blanch in boiling water for 1 minute then shock in cold water. Squeeze excess water from spinach and saute with garlic in butter and olive oil until spinach just begins to wilt. Season to taste and serve immediately.

Shrimp or Fish Stock

1/4 cup melted butter
3/4 lb shrimp and/or lobster shells
1/2 onion
1 celery stalk
1/2 carrot
1-1/2 cups sherry
1-1/2 quarts water

Saute shells in butter until crisped and brightly colored. Rough chop onion, celery, carrot and add with remaining ingredients. Gently simmer for 20 minutes and strain.

Variation: For a fish stock, use white fish bones instead of shells and replace sherry with white wine.

Grilled Pineapple Relish

1 ripe pineapple
1/2 cup vegetable oil
1/2 red bell pepper
1/2 green bell pepper
1/2 small onion
1 tsp chopped garlic

4 scallions, chopped
1/2 tomato, diced
1 tsp chopped fresh thyme
2 tblsps chopped fresh cilantro
1/4 tsp black pepper
1/4 cup rice vinegar

Peel and cut pineapple into 1/2 inch slices. Sear in hot oil or grill until browned to bring out sugar. Core and dice slices. Cut the peppers and onion into chunks. Saute with garlic in vegetable oil until soft. Combine with diced pineapple and all remaining ingredients. Mix well and serve warm or cold.

Potato Pancakes

3 medium to large potatoes, washed
1 medium onion, peeled
1/2 cup milk
2 tblsps flour
1 egg
1 tblsp chopped fresh chives or parsley
salt & pepper to taste
vegetable oil for frying

Hand shred the potatoes and onion using a fine size grater. In a bowl, combine the potatoes and onion with the remaining ingredients. Liberally coat a cast iron skillet or nonstick pan with oil. Heat the oil until <u>very</u> hot. Spoon potato mixture into skillet, forming cakes 3 to 4 inches in diameter. Cook for 3 minutes on each side until browned and center is cooked through.

Index

TradeWinds Island Resorts
wishes to thank each of the chefs whose talents and
service enhance the beach experience for our guests, especially
Food & Beverage Director and Executive Chef Jeffrey Fredrickson.

First Published in the U.S.A. by Espichel Enterprises
Recipes and Food Design: Chef Jeffrey Fredrickson
Managing Editor: Susan Eanes
Photography & Design: Charles Eanes
Produced by: Lynda Waters
All photographs were taken on location at TradeWinds Island Resorts

Library of Congress Control Number: 2005937471
ISBN 1-890494-11-9   Printed in the U.S.A.
Copyright© 2005 by TradeWinds Island Resorts

TradeWinds
ISLAND RESORTS ON ST. PETE BEACH
5600 Gulf Boulevard
St. Pete Beach, Florida 33706
866-JustLetGo 727-363-2215
www.JustLetGo.com